THE LICE OF CHRIST

Bill Yarrow

MadHat Press
Asheville, North Carolina

MadHat Press
MadHat Incorporated
PO Box 8364, Asheville, NC 28814

The Library of Congress has assigned
this edition a Control Number of
2014930597

ISBN 978-0-9885490-8-1 (paperback)

Cover art by Eryk Wenziak
Book and cover design by MadHat Press

www.madhat-press.com

For Alexander Graubart

"I call Poet he who picks the lice off Christ"

—Adolphus of Smyrna
The Incanteron

CONTENTS

ONE

8 NEW WAYS OF LOOKING AT WAFFLES

1. the mind (in its righteousness)
waffles

2. the conscience (in its scrupulousness)
waffles

3. the heart (in its cupidity)
waffles

4. the soul (in its annihilation)
waffles

5. the tongue (in its appeasement)
waffles

6. the skin (in its lethargy)
waffles

7. the body (in its luxury)
waffles

8. life (in its delirium)
waffles

Bill Yarrow

THEORIZING SALSA

Janet and I
had the tilapia
fish tacos and
talked about God

God ordered the veal
cutlet and was rebuked
by the vegetarian Politburo

The beer had a divine odor which
attracted the wasps of mortuary remorse

SATAN AND THE MOON

1.
Satan and the moon | are made of cheese.
That's what my wife | taught my kids.
They all | dropped out of school.

2.
Study decay. | Don't mollify
the obvious. | Watch TV but only
at the full. At solstice | turn it off.

3.
Patrician vicissitudes | run ransack
with benign alignments | of the brain.
Never never never | feed the publicans.

POEM FOR DANNY

sometimes you're camping in Wisconsin
thinking about Melville and wondering
what he'd make of Nat King Cole

and sometimes you're on a job in Idaho
and you hear the pop of cooking soup
but there's nothing in the microwave

and sometimes you're in Lubbock
in a hotel filled with polished apples
and carts of recovered luggage

and sometimes you're in Boca Raton
in the company of salesmen
whose wives died of complications

and sometimes you're in Park City
harried as a lariat
lonely as a coati

and sometimes you're in Park Slope
staring from a convention window
at girders so innocent they seem almost botanic

and sometimes floating in the Gulf of Mexico
you close your eyes and let the water cover them
and then for a time which seems like mercy

you don't know where you are
or remember where you were
or imagine where you may go

DALI'S TEMPTATION OF ST ANTHONY

temptatioN always   as hairy algebrA

             comes to us

    in   our   rancid

             nakedneSS

  we   can   offer

bacK   only the fractured   geometrY

           icons of radiant

JUGULAR MOON

he packs his assault rifle in his valise
just in case there are rabid cats in Cannes

he sleeps with his back to the exit
as a precaution against inadvertency

he motions to the stewardess for help
then realizes they are no longer aloft

he maneuvers the wheelchair out of the way
of the disabled man to whom it belongs

he walks upon the beach with sand shoes
as if that makes any difference to the maid

he gulps his last dinner with nervous fervor
hoping that choking might land him on TV

walking on the runway toward the waiting plane
he sees the future as a tracking shot

GETTING HOME ALIVE

he enters

> the pavilion
>> from the left
> and surveys

the indigo walls

in the alcove

> by the pond
>> scarlet shadows
> thatch

the empty bench

in a grove

> of dying
>> birch trees
> a wasp loses focus

a sniper coughs

Bill Yarrow

SOMETHING, HE WROTE

Mayakovsky wrote

> in the cathedral
>   of my heart
> the choir
>   is on fire

I love those lines
I just never realized
he was talking about

arson

TWO

(

ADDICTIONS

- There is much more alcoholism in the world than there is alcohol.
- The women in the Women's Christian Temperance Union were all drunks. They were drunk on the idea of being in the W.C.T.U.
- Exercise: an intoxicant like any other.
- Immaturity: an addiction like any other.
- Those intoxicated by art or God never admit their alcoholism.
- One can be addicted to tofu as well as opium.
- Obsession: a hobby on heroin.
- Pleasure is the addictive ingredient in all repeated behavior.
- The hierarchy of pleasure is always idiosyncratic.
- As our pleasures stagnate or evolve, so do our addictions.
- Our pleasure thermostat is set in youth.
- Over time, pleasures congeal.
- The body builds in itself powerful pleasures—excretion, sneezing, rest.
- Pleasure fuels the engine of life.
- Some pleasures are more pleasurable than others. If public service were more pleasurable than cocaine, people would be addicted to public service.
- All advertising is an appeal to pleasure and a warning about pain. Prostitutes, blackmailers, drug pushers, and extortionists mentor the advertisers and teach them their trade.
- Marketing: psychology for capitalists.
- Selling comfort is still selling.

- How hypocritical of capitalism to condemn monopoly and profiteering. Profiteering is the point of capitalism, monopoly its goal.
- In order to be masters, people so desire money that, to acquire it, they consent to being slaves.
- It's the twenty-first century and we still have maids and waiters and doormen and drivers and guards and caretakers and house painters and tutors and shoeblacks and prostitutes. Why? Because money is still the fuel and hegemony is still the car.
- You can try to go through life with clean hands, but you do so at the price of your soul.
- The evil of money is that it allows us to forsake our human duties.
- Slavery can be legislated against but it can never be abolished. We're no longer slaves to human owners, but we're still slaves to our desires, our fears, our histories, our ideals, and our genes.
- There's no significant difference between the kid in fourth grade who was willing to lick a dirty floor for a quarter and the employee who is willing to do anything to keep his job.
- If there's a collective unconscious, there are also collective addictions.
- Standing in a crowd: addiction by association.
- The mob intoxicates. The opiate is the people.

EVERYTHING MOLTEN DESERVES A MOLD

- Everything molten deserves a mold. Passion is molten. Passion's mold is art.
- Art is the pin in the butterfly of life.
- Art is alchemy, turning life (lead) into art (gold).
- Art is tidy; life is incoherent.
- Art believes in stable identity, but no living personality is coherent. Therefore, art falsifies the living in order to approximate life.
- Personal taste or predilection has no place in the construction of a definition or building a philosophy. In defining art, for example, it's a mistake to assume that everything you like is art and must fit into your definition. I like very much the caffeinated manifesti of Tzara and Marinetti, the mad randomness of Smart and Huidobro, the mannered fragmentation of Barbellion and Traherne, the epistolary brilliance of Byron and Henry Miller, but why must my definition of art have to include everything I like? Why must my definition of art exclude my tepid affections—Wharton or Turgenev or James? The reasons I like and do not like specific works or writers are quite separate from my ideas about what makes art.
- The great enemy of art is taste.
- Hell is a library with only one book: *The Ambassadors.*
- Tastes change. What was beautiful in one age is considered beautiful no longer. The great problem of art criticism is how to recapture a historical sense of beauty.
- The sordid: a legitimate subject for art. There can be sordid art, but there can be no such thing as ugly art.

- When one talks about ugly art, one means repulsive art, sordid art. Art and ugliness are incompatible. Ugly is a handling, not a subject.
- One can say with absolute conviction that a painting is ugly but only if one means that the painting is artistically incompetent.
- Art is order; ugliness is disorder.
- Without form, into what will you pour your genius?
- Things too neat are also untrue.
- A perfect face is not an interesting face. Cosmetic surgeons understand only perfection. If you wanted to improve your appearance, you'd be better off going to a cosmetic artist.
- We live in a pornographic world, a world in which we watch the movement of football players in football games, the mien and posture of fashion models, study sociology abstracted from history and literature, biology disembodied of theology and geometry, astronomy absent from music and architecture. The impulse for pornography is the impulse for isolation, that is to say, separate study. All focused observation, all specialization, is pornographic. Pornography is rooted in seeing the thing, whatever it happens to be, in isolation. Pornography is anything that focuses on the part to the exclusion of the whole.
- Pornography is the metonymy of vision.
- Awareness isn't an infinite good.
- The shocking, the absurd, the uncanny, the grotesque, the sublime—these are the drugs of art. We have to keep upping the ante to regain the rush.
- We teach ourselves our talent. We train our minds to think as artists, to think as builders, to think as poets, to think as salesman, to think as managers, to think as lawmakers, to think as teachers. We train our minds to think in stories, in

sales, in scenes, in structures, in images, in lectures, in ideas, in jokes, in designs, in colors, in formulae, in equations, in slogans, in insights.

- In great art, we watch the artist's thinking unfold. In the greatest art, we watch our own thinking unfold.
- Great art is like an attack of smallpox. After it inhabits the body, it leaves a permanent scar.
- When I reread a book or reexamine an artwork, I revisit the person I once was.
- The beginning of understanding is observation.
- Observation is learned.
- Real understanding always comes as a tear in the tissue.
- There's no mending the breakthrough.
- Everything artistic partakes of beauty. Sordidness of presentation, foul subject matter, repellent ideology be damned. Swift. Celine. George Grosz. Otto Dix. Leni Riefenstahl. Ivan Albrecht. Diane Arbus. Robert Mapplethorpe. Nan Goldin. Lolita.
- Art is an ideological whore who'll sleep with any propaganda or point of view. That's why there can be religious art, capitalist art, socialist art, racist art.
- Art: a promiscuous mistress. Leni Riefenstahl is no different from Piero della Francesca or Giotto. The great Catholic art of the Renaissance is just the other side of despicable political propaganda.
- God vs. Satan. In other words, art vs. crap.
- We learn by repetition, but what do we worship? Novelty.
- When the future becomes obsessed with the better, the past begins to be extinguished as the worse.
- The interesting begins in the absurd, but it doesn't end there.

- The dark edge of the profound is silly: Meister Eckhart, Swedenborg, Madame Blavatsky.
- The dark edge of the silly is profound: Edward Lear, Lewis Carroll, Calvino.
- People are afraid of artworks having only one meaning as if that were somehow autocratic. Complex works of art have complex meanings. Complex doesn't mean multiple.
- Meaning does not change. Understanding of meaning changes.
- Misunderstanding is also understanding.
- The clearer one's sense of self, the sharper one's vision.
- Only the mason has the deepest understanding of the imperfections of his wall.
- Literature is a vanity mirror. We stare into another person's soul and see only ourselves.
- There is the imagination of the creator and there is the imagination of the audience. They are antagonists.
- The purpose of literature is not to set us dreaming but to discipline our dreams.

GETTING GODLESS

I.

- God is man squared. That is to say, God is man raised to a higher power.
- Man is the root, the square root, of God.
- We believe in the ideal (truth, wisdom, justice, honor, integrity, selflessness, sacrifice, compassion, goodness) and God is the name we give to that ideal.
- What else is God but a heuristic for what we want to do with our lives?
- The worship of God is the worship of perfection. The perfection of space: infinity. The perfection of time: eternity. The perfection of power: omnipotence. The perfection of knowledge: omniscience. The perfection of behavior: virtue.
- Since the Fall, falling is what we've learned to do.
- We are blemished perfections.
- Man is the asymptote of what he predicates God to be.
- We define ourselves by what we are trying not to be. Some men try to be men by not being womanly. Some women try to be women by not being manly. Some men try to be men by not being too manly. Some women try to be women by not being too womanly. People assert their humanness by differentiating it from brutishness. Man posits God's divinity in contradistinction to humanity.
- Science teaches us that there is no one thing in the world, that everything is made of smaller and smaller substances. God's indivisibility draws a line in the sand against science.
- Dostoyevsky said that without God, everything is permitted. Behind that statement is the correct notion that with God, anything can be prohibited.
- God can be seen in man's ability to imagine God.

II.

- We don't buy into God; we marry into Him.
- Agnosticism: a philosophical position built not on belief or doubt but on an inability to decide.
- An agnostic is a tepid thing, a spineless thing, a bowl of mush.
- The deists were atheists without the courage of their convictions.
- Modern religion: carpe deism.
- The atheist can't stop thinking about God. The religious man can't stop thinking about atheism.
- The first millennium was a fight for freedom of religion. The second millennium is a fight for freedom from religion.

III.

- Jealousy is a cocktail made of equal parts insecurity and possession.
- Before we can be jealous, we must make our mate our thing.
- Our God is a jealous God. What an unfortunate idea.
- The God fantasy infantilizes man.
- God likes being happy. God insists on being happy. He's told us so. So is God smiling or frowning? That's what every religious war's about.
- Suggestiveness is not a god.
- Religion scares the hell out of people by scaring Hell into people.
- What hardens thought into belief? Corroboration.
- Religion is division.
- Religion isn't about spirituality—it's about ritual.
- What begins as respect too often ends as worship.

IV.
- Amulets. Lucky charms. God.
- Overseers. Consciences. God.
- Kings. Fathers. God.
- Policemen. Judges. God.
- Teachers. Authors. God.
- Accountants. Engineers. God.
- God—the Great Excuse.
- God—the Seatbelt of the Soul.
- Personal trainers. Personal bankers. Personal gods.
- God: a godforsaken construct.
- Heraclitus for God.

V.
- Vengeance is mine, saith the Lord. God is Love. Same God.
- The Lord will rain for ever and ever, and, on that day, the Earth shall be wet and His name wet.
- All magic look real. We are desperate to believe, but how can we? It's all sham. Embrace sham. Squeeze tight. It'll shatter and the world will be honest again.
- Numerology derives its meaning from manipulation. It's no less deceitful and no less entrancing than magic.
- Spirituality is a shell game.

VI.
- The divine is our great wish. There's nothing objective about a wish.
- Prayer is affirmation of belief. Prayer with the expectation of a response is absurd beyond belief.
- Wishes are not real, but wishing is real. Dreams are not real, but dreaming is real. Thoughts are not real, but thinking is real. Belief is not real, but believing is real. The world is full

31

of wishes, dreams, thoughts, and beliefs embodied, made real.

- As Jesus embodies sacrifice, as Buddha embodies renunciation, so God embodies meaning.
- I am the dream of my parents embodied. Everyone is a dream made real.
- There is no difference in effect between false belief and true belief. The effect of any belief is always positive.
- What is efficacious in belief systems is not the object of the belief (i.e. Jesus or Buddha) but belief itself. Believing in something is worthwhile even if the something is false.
- Reality exists independent of our perception of it; on the other hand, reality does not exist *for us* independent of our perception of it.
- God is a cosmic placebo.

VII.
- Religion exists to oppose the incursions of time.
- The odds don't always favor the house, but in the long run the house always wins.
- The Devil lives in the house.
- A religious leader is a vanity mirror for his congregation.
- Christian morality is the drawing of lines; it's a geometry. Judaism draws fences and is concerned with the area under the curve; it's a calculus. Taoism is string theory.
- Judeo-Christianity: Zoroastrianism in a tuxedo.
- The population of the world accepts unthinkingly the rightness of the religion or the atheism it is born into.
- You want to worship the ideal (call it God), you want to believe it possible—go ahead. If it stretches you, if it makes you live up to something, great. Just don't smear it with the bullshit of personification and intentionality and intervention.

VIII.
- People are desperate to posit a soul—they need something to blame their good impulses on.
- The soul is a pilot light. When the light goes out, we inflate with combustible soullessness.
- Science's biological and chemical refutation of the mind/body split has killed the concept of soul in man. The death of the soul freed man from the fetters of shame.
- If science really wants to understand spirituality and mysticism, it should begin by unraveling the phenomenon of feeling being looked at by people behind us, the phenomenon of feeling eyes on the back of our necks.
- I don't believe in spirits or a spirit realm. I do, however, believe in thought. The brain is uncontained by the skull. Its waves leak out and interfere in the world. Ghosts, called spirits, are, more precisely, the coalescence of leaked thinking.
- Exhaustion of the body frees the mind to wander in the spirit.
- Soul—a comforting delusion.

IX.
- The person who eats his vegetables first is not morally superior to the person who eats his vegetables last.
- There's no virtue that can't be vulgarized. Just as there are gourmets in eating, there are also gourmands in defecation.
- Depravity doesn't evolve; it mutates.
- Virtue can never be habitual. Goodness is always a function of will.
- Utility is always a value, but awareness isn't an infinite good.
- An ethics of expedience, not of obligation.
- There are accomplices to virtuous acts as well as to crimes.

What, in basketball, is called an assist, in morality, is called virtuous complicity.

- Integrity, indistinguishable from intransigence or recalcitrance, is just a more exalted form of perversity.
- The moral man brings up phlegm but does not spit it out.

X.

- Cause murks the morality.
- Relativism is the philosophical justification of deviance.
- To eliminate deviance, eliminate absolutes. For Dostoyevsky, the Absolute was the same as God. *If God does not exist, then everything is permitted*, he said.
- Morality relies on observation. God is watching, the police are watching, my neighbors are watching. It's solitude that allows and enables sin.
- If you want to construct a moral society, construct one where people are always in each other's presence.
- *I'm OK, you're OK* is the sniveling Laertes saying, *Exchange forgiveness with me, Hamlet.* I'll let you off the hook if you let me off the hook.
- Morality is not a quid pro quo. Morality is washing our own dirty backs. *You wash my back and I'll wash yours* is no different from *You wash my backside and I'll wash yours.* The only difference is, in the second instance, the disgusting nature of the transaction is made transparent.
- *Do unto others as you would have others do unto you.* Quid pro blowjob.
- Morality is a refraining from, not an indulging in.

XI.

- Understanding is dangerous because it results, inevitably, in forgiveness.

- Forgiveness is a function of understanding. Understanding is the secret tunnel that runs directly from the head to the heart.
- Empathy is denial of conscience, vilification of judgment.
- Empathy is a form of enabling. It says, *Yes, yes, yes! I know what you mean. I understand how you feel.* Empathy is part of the conspiracy to make all ideas, all beliefs, all feelings equal.
- Empathy results in exculpation. It results in: "O Doctor Mengele, you poor man!"
- Forgiveness is no virtue. It's the beginning of vice.

XII.
- Before genetics, there were gods.
- Heredity, environment, and culture: the modern determinist gods.
- Gregor Mendel reinvented fate.
- Everyone alive is an exemplar of a triumphant fitness.
- The debate between Athens and Sparta was really a unified argument in favor of nurture over nature, in favor of the environment over heredity.
- What's providence for one person is deliberation for someone else. The Corinthian messenger's volition tastes like fate to Oedipus.
- Luck is the name we give to unwilled repetition.
- The crosses and the stars you wear—magic amulets—to protect yourself from yourself.
- Superstition is the name we give to the spurious cause of a legitimate effect.
- The greatest superstition is a belief in providence or grace.

XIII.

- Who invented virtue—I say the Devil.
- Who invented coherence—I say the Devil.
- Who invented pity—I say the Devil.
- Who invented forgiveness—I say the Devil.
- Who invented reward—I say the Devil.
- Who invented hope—I say the Devil.
- Who invented religion—I say the Devil.
- Who invented the Devil? Religion.

THREE

BABBLE

We had a family copy of Isaac Babel's
stories out of which my dad would read
aloud when he was home, which owing
to his employment issues was very often.
I had no idea what I was listening to, but
that's just another way to fail to define
childhood, I guess. Anyway, the stories
were short, some just a page, and I let
my imagination sail away on some word
that jumped out at me (one always did)
and then, for those few minutes, I was
outside the battered gates of self, alone
in a city empty of rockets and God, where
I saw tower after tower of arrested escape.

THE KNITTING NEEDLE

It was early in the morning when Lucien Carr stabbed
David Kammerer in the chest with a Boy Scout knife,
dropped the knife into a sewer, the body in the river,
and buried the dead man's glasses in the park.

It was later that afternoon when Lucien Carr
went to see *The Four Feathers* with Jack Kerouac,
walked to the Museum of Modern Art to look at the Legers
and turned himself in to the skeptical police.

It was a grey afternoon when Lucien Carr
holding a torn copy of *A Vision* by William Butler Yeats
pled guilty to first-degree manslaughter
and was sentenced to a reformatory in Elmira, New York.

The odor of William Blake hangs over this narrative.
Opposition is true friendship. Eternity in an hour.

HELIX POEM (Samuel Johnson / James Joyce)

sorrow
  gazing up
is a kind
  into the blackness
of rust
  I saw myself
of the soul
  as a creature
which
  driven and derided
every new idea
  by vanity
contributes
  and my eyes burned
in its passage
  with anguish
to scour
  and anger
away

JOHN OF GOD (Painted by Murillo, 1672)

pictures a kneeling man in a monk's robe
lifting a naked beggar onto his shoulder

a bright light coming from the upper left
corner of the canvas attracts his attention

turning he sees a dark-haired winged boy
in a gold dress stretch out his arm in aid

NO ONE CAN BE A BASTARD FOREVER

THIS IS NOT A POEM
for René Magritte

When the preacher's dog got into the motor oil
in the alley and tore through the hotel lobby,
the aged concierge at his fluid heels, the town
predicted Tom Allen would win a Pulitzer Prize
for the story he would write for the local paper.

But Tom did not win the Pulitzer Prize because
Tom could not write that story because no oil-
stained dog tore through the hotel lobby because
there was no discarded motor oil in the alley
and the preacher, being allergic, had no dog.

No preacher. No dog. No town. No people of the town.
No hotel. No hotel lobby. No aged concierge. No local
paper. No Tom Allen. Just the viral thought of him.

Bill Yarrow

NOT A VILLANELLE

screams in the blonde
polyp air then peroxide
nausea pushing up
ringed fingers tarpaulin
tested flesh moldy rose
perfume privileged tits
porcelain privacy surprise

porcelain privacy surprise
perfume privileged tits
tested flesh moldy rose
ringed fingers tarpaulin
nausea pushing up
polyp air then peroxide
screams in the blonde

FINLAND

When in doubt, walk around the world.
When in doubt, blacken the i's in the dictionary.
When in doubt, ask tobacco.
When in doubt, hack a tree.
When in doubt, preen like Dietrich.
When in doubt, pretend to make love.

Love, let us be faithless to one another.
Let plate tectonics have the day. Let's
drink to BPA and zombiefy ambition.
Let's smoke a pot roast, mainline a
mango, snort a mortgage, shoplift a kiss.
Let's inculcate. Let's make baptism a sin.

She: You're cute in a Jean Sibelius kind of way.
He: I'd go out with you but your Google profile is so unattractive.

Bill Yarrow

The Separation

wrote yeats: *the intellect of man*
is forced to choose

perfection of the art   *or of the life*

who was yeats to posit that separation?

I pondered yeats   I pondered my heart
 I pondered my past   I pondered my children
I pondered my marriage   I pondered my future

I concluded

life is rich pudding   life is rough soup

WHAT A MONSTER I WOULD HAVE BECOME HAD I GONE THROUGH LIFE UNIMPEDED

the
title
of
this
poem
is
far
better
than
this
naked
 snake
of
words

ACKNOWLEDGMENTS

"8 New Ways of Looking at Waffles" in *Gloom Cupboard*
"Addictions" in *PANK*
"Babble" in *fwriction : review*
"Dali's Temptation of St. Anthony" in *Up the Staircase*
"Everything Molten Deserves a Mold" in *PANK* as
      "Convictions"
"Finland" in *Mad Hatters' Review*
"Getting Godless" in *PANK*, reprinted in *Novembre*
"Getting Home Alive" in *Negative Suck*
"Helix Poem" in *Blue Five Notebook*
"John of God" in *Blue Five Notebook*
"Jugular Moon" in *Lost in Thought*
"Not a Villanelle" in *Literary Orphans*
"Poem for Danny" in *Scissors & Spackle*
"Satan and the Moon" in *Used Furniture Review*
"Something, He Wrote" in *Angelic Dynamo*
"The Knitting Needle" in *Blue Fifth Review*
"The Separation" in *Otoliths*
"Theorizing Salsa" in *PANK*
"This is Not a Poem" in *Otoliths*
"What a Monster I Would Have Become Had I Gone through
      Life Unimpeded" in *Short, Fast, and Deadly*

ABOUT THE AUTHOR

Bill Yarrow is the author of *Pointed Sentences* (BlazeVOX, 2012) and *Incompetent Translations and Inept Haiku* (Červená Barva Press, 2013). His poems have appeared in many print and online magazines including *Treehouse, Contrary, RHINO, PANK,* and *DIAGRAM.*